EDGE BOOKS

NATURE'S INVADERS

KEEP OUT!

INVASIVE SPECIES

BY SARA L. LATTA

CAPSTONE PRESS
a capstone imprint

Edge Books are published by Capstone Press,
1710 Roe Crest Drive, North Mankato, Minnesota 56003
www.capstonepub.com

Library of Congress Cataloging-in-Publication Data
Latta, Sara L.
Keep out! : invasive species / by Sara L. Latta.
p. cm.—(Edge books. Nature's invaders)
Summary: "A look at invasive species, including how they affect other species and
what can be done to prevent them from spreading"—Provided by publisher.
Audience: 008-014.
Audience: Grades 4 to 6.
Includes bibliographical references and index.
ISBN 978-1-4765-0140-6 (library binding)
ISBN 978-1-4765-3394-0 (eBook PDF)
1. Introduced organisms—Juvenile literature. 2. Biological invasions—Juvenile
literature. I. Title.
QH353.L38 2014
578.62—dc23   2013005604

Editorial Credits
Anthony Wacholtz, editor; Ted Williams, designer; Jo Miller, media researcher;
Eric Manske, production specialist

Photo Credits
Alamy: Jim West, 7; Corbis: Visuals Unlimited/Alex Wild, 13; iStockphotos: Kevin
Herrin, 3 (ants), 12 (inset); Newscom: ZUMA Press/Detroit Free Press/Brian
Kaufman, cover (fish); Shutterstock: Ackab Photography, 20-21 (flock), Arie v.d.
Wolde, 3 (flowers), Arthur van der Kooij, cover (bird), Bara22, 18-19, cellistka, cover
(snake), darios, 22 (bottom), David Huntley, 9, Deborah Benbrook, 1, Heiko Kiera,
3 (snake), 5, Reddogs, 21 (bird), Trent Townsend, 10 (snake); US Fish and Wildlife
Service, 15; USDA photo by Bob Nichols, 28, Grace Lentini, 3 (man), Monica Errico,
27; Wikimedia: James Gathany, CDC, 25, Scott Bauer, USDA Agricultural Research
Service, 3 (bees), 22 (top), Jacob Hoefnagel, 10 (dodo), S.Koilraj, 17

Design Elements
Shutterstock: dcwcreations, foxie, happykanppy, JohnySima, jumpingsack, Michal
Ninger, sdecoret

Printed in the United States of America in Stevens Point, Wisconsin.
032013   007227WZF13

TABLE OF CONTENTS

CHAPTER ONE

THE INVADERS ARE COMING!

An alligator suns itself in the shallow waters of the Florida Everglades. Nearby, a hungry snake watches and waits. The snake swims closer. Lightning-fast, it strikes. Razor-sharp teeth clamp down on the alligator's head. The snake wraps its powerful body around the alligator and swallows the beast whole.

This story may sound like a scary movie, but it's true. For thousands of years, the American alligator was one of the top **predators** in the Everglades. But a newcomer threatens to take its place: the Burmese python. It is one of the world's largest snakes. It can grow longer than 25 feet (7.6 meters) and weigh close to 300 pounds (136 kilograms). It is not **native** to Florida, but to Southeast Asia.

How did the pythons reach Florida? Some were pets that escaped or were released by their owners when they became too big. Others wriggled away from pet shops after a hurricane in 1992. Scientists estimate that there are at least 10,000 wild pythons in the Everglades National Park.

The Burmese pythons have scientists worried. These snakes have huge appetites. For them, the Everglades is one big all-you-can-eat buffet. They have nearly wiped out many native mammals in the area, including raccoons, bobcats, rabbits, and foxes.

✳ **predator**—an animal that hunts other animals for food

✳ **native**—describes a species that lives and grows naturally in a particular region without the help of humans

Invaders Fact

The Everglades is a huge area of land and water in southern Florida. One nickname for it is "The River of Grass."

● Burmese pythons can be hard to spot amongst the sticks and plants in the Everglades.

WHAT ARE INVASIVE SPECIES?

From the Florida Everglades to the Australian Outback, animals, plants, and even **microbes** are showing up in places where they don't belong. These invaders have found their way from their natural **ecosystems** to new homes. They harm the environment and cost people money. They may even pose a risk to human health. They are called invasive **species**.

Species that are introduced to a new ecosystem may not have any natural predators. They can breed and spread quickly. They can eat native species that do not have defenses against the new invaders. They compete with native species for food and habitat. Some cause new diseases.

Humans are most often responsible for bringing invasive species to their new homes. Sometimes people bring them in for a specific purpose. Other invasive species are accidental hitchhikers.

* **microbe**—a living thing that is too small to see without a microscope

* **ecosystem**—a system of living and nonliving things in an environment

* **species**—a group of living things that share common characteristics

FRIENDLY NEWCOMERS

Invasive species are likely to cause harm to the habitat or to the native species. But not all species that are introduced to new ecosystems are harmful. They may even be good for the area. Corn, wheat, rice, cattle, and horses are just a few of the helpful species that people have brought to the United States.

• Zebra mussels first appeared in the United States in 1988. The invasive species became a pest in the Great Lakes.

CHAPTER TWO

LAND INVADERS

Across the southern part of the United States, a plant called kudzu creeps up telephone poles. It smothers other plants and wraps around trees. The weight of its vines can cause entire buildings to collapse. In the summer, the weed can grow 1 foot (0.3 meter) every day. No wonder some people call kudzu the "vine that ate the South."

Kudzu came to the United States from its native home in Asia in 1876. At first, people planted it because its pretty purple flowers smelled like grapes. It provided shade from the hot sun. Farmers found that their cattle liked kudzu, so they planted more. People also noticed that kudzu's strong, spreading roots prevented heavy rainfalls from washing away the soil. So they planted even more.

The vine thrived in the mild winters and hot summers of its new home. It had no natural enemies, so it spread quickly. By 1972 the "miracle vine" had become a weed.

- Kudzu can grow up to 60 feet (18 m) during one growing season.

Invaders Fact

People in many Asian countries have been making herbal medicines from kudzu for thousands of years.

Kudzu is hard to kill. Chemical weed killers do not work very well on it. Chemicals can also harm the environment. Some cities have come up with a solution. They buy herds of kudzu-gobbling goats and sheep. When the animals finish clearing one spot, they move to another area. However, kudzu continues to be a problem. The goats and sheep cannot keep up with the large numbers of kudzu in the South.

• Brown tree snakes are usually 3 to 6 feet (0.9 to 1.8 m) long. But some of the brown tree snakes on Guam have grown to be 10 feet (3 m) long.

BROWN TREE SNAKE

In 1983 scientists visiting the tiny Pacific island of Guam noticed something strange. The dense forest in the U.S. island territory was silent. No birds sang. The scientists were puzzled. Where had the birds gone?

The scientists soon found the problem. Many years before, the brown tree snake had somehow hitched a ride to Guam. The New Guinea native might have arrived in the cargo area of an airplane or ship. For years, the snakes slithered through the trees. They snuck into bird nests and ate the eggs and chicks. The native birds had no defense against these new predators. With plenty of food and no natural enemies, the number of brown tree snakes grew. Today scientists estimate there are as many as 13,000 brown tree snakes per 1 square mile (2.6 square kilometers) on Guam.

Many forest-dwelling bird species native to Guam have been wiped out. With so few birds left, the numbers of insects and spiders has soared. Now the brown tree snake has turned to eating the island's lizards, frogs, and small mammals. Two of the island's species of bats may be extinct.

The snakes also cause other problems. They slither onto high-voltage cables, creating short circuits and damage. Officials are working hard to make sure the pests don't make their way to other islands.

extinct—no longer living; an extinct animal is one that has died out, with no more of its kind

RED IMPORTED FIRE ANT

Anyone who has ever been stung by a red imported fire ant knows how it got its name. The sting burns like fire! The fire ant hitched a ride on a cargo ship from its home in South America to Mobile, Alabama, in the 1930s. From there it has spread across many states, including Texas and states on the southeastern coast.

ANT EATERS

Scientists have imported one of the fire ants' natural predators from South America to combat the problems they cause. The predator is a tiny fly that injects its eggs into the ant. The fly **larvae**, or maggots, hatch a couple of weeks later. They worm their way into the head of the ant. About two weeks later, each maggot releases a chemical that causes the ant's head to fall off. The maggots eat the ant's brain and complete their development in the safety of the ant's head.

Red imported fire ants are more likely to attack their prey than fire ants native to the United States. The ants will eat just about anything, plants and animals alike. They swarm onto animals and sting all at once. Some people have even died from fire ant attacks.

For unknown reasons, they are attracted to electrical systems. They invade air conditioners, traffic lights, and airport runway lights. They gnaw on wires, causing short circuits and loss of power.

• Fire ants live in colonies. Each colony contains between 100,000 and 500,000 ants.

larva—an insect at the stage of development between an egg and an adult; larvae is plural for larva

CHAPTER THREE
AQUATIC INVADERS

In the 1970s a catfish farmer in the United States brought several species of Asian carp into the country to help keep his pond water clean. The carp eat algae and other tiny creatures, and they have huge appetites. They can eat as much as their body weight each day. The carp can grow to be more than 4 feet (1.2 m) long and weigh more than 100 pounds (45 kg). Its smaller cousin, the silver carp, tops out at just over 3 feet (1 m) long and a weight of 60 pounds (27 kg).

The Asian carp likely escaped their ponds during floods in the 1980s. The fish found their way to the Mississippi River and rivers that connect to it. Their numbers grew rapidly in the rivers. Today they are starving out native fish that eat the same kind of food. In some stretches of the Illinois River, up to nine out of 10 fish are Asian carp.

Wildlife biologists and fishermen fear that the carp will invade the Great Lakes. The invaders could destroy the region's $7 billion fishing industry. Engineers have built electrical fish barriers on the canal connecting the Illinois River to Lake Michigan to keep them out.

WATER HYACINTH

Water gardeners in New Orleans discovered the water hyacinth in 1884. They loved its glossy green leaves and pretty purple flowers. Soon the South American native floated on ponds across the southern United States.

But the plants grow fast—very fast! Just two small plants can produce 1,200 more plants in only two months. When the young plants break free, wind or water currents help them form new colonies. They can quickly cover entire lakes, rivers, and canals. They can form mats dense enough for people to walk on.

Today the water hyacinth is causing problems all around the world. It costs some countries in Asia and Africa more than $100 million each year. The plants block waterways and clog pumps. They kill underwater native plants by blocking sunlight and oxygen. Fish and other water animals also die because they can't get enough oxygen.

Invaders Fact

It is difficult to get rid of water hyacinths once they have invaded an area. People are experimenting with new ways to harvest and use the plants. For example, the dried plants can be used to make baskets.

● If water hyacinth is not controlled, it can creep outward across a body of water.

Nutria carry a parasite that can infect human skin. The parasite causes a rash called "nutria itch."

NUTRIA

The nutria looks like a cross between a beaver and rat. Nutria have thick brown hair, long white whiskers, and orange teeth. The species has invaded marshes and wetlands in 17 or more U.S. states. The South American native eats the tender roots of marsh grasses, leaving behind vast mudflats. Nutria destroy the habitat for fish, birds, and other animals that live in the wetlands. Their burrows can weaken dams and break down the banks of streams and lakes. Nutria have destroyed thousands of acres of marsh in the United States.

People brought nutria to the United States in 1899 for their fur. Nutria fur coats and hats were popular for a time, but people stopped buying them in the 1940s. Fur farmers could no longer afford to feed their nutria, so they released them into the wild. Other nutria escaped during storms and floods.

People are trying to keep the nutria population under control by killing or trapping the animals. Some fashion designers are even trying to get people interested in wearing nutria coats again.

CHAPTER FOUR

FLYING INVADERS

In 1890 and 1891, New Yorker Eugene Schieffel released 100 European starlings into New York City's Central Park. He wanted to introduce every bird mentioned by poet William Shakespeare to North America. Some birds, such as the skylarks and song thrushes, did not survive. But the starlings were wildly successful. Today more than 200 million starlings live throughout North America.

Starlings gather in flocks of up to 1 million. In cities, their droppings coat buildings and sidewalks. Around airports, flocks of starlings sometimes fly straight into airplanes, causing the planes' engines to fail. Farmers dislike starlings because they devour crops. The birds also take over the nesting places of native birds, including woodpeckers and bluebirds.

People try to scare the birds away. They use loud firecrackers, water sprays, or flashing lights. People also blast the birds' "danger" call over loudspeakers.

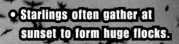
● **Starlings often gather at sunset to form huge flocks.**

Invaders Fact

The starling is about the size of a robin. It has glossy black feathers that sometimes shine purple and green. The feathers develop white spots in the fall and winter.

AFRICANIZED HONEYBEE

In 1956 scientists in Brazil imported honeybees from Africa. They were brought in to **pollinate** crops. But the African honeybees did not do well in the warm parts of South America. The scientists hoped they could create a different honeybee that would thrive and produce more honey. A year later some of the African honeybees escaped. They mated with the native European honeybees, producing a hybrid called the Africanized honeybee. The hybrids produced less honey than the European honeybees, but they thrived—all too well.

The Africanized honeybee (left) is similar in appearance to the European honeybee (right).

The hybrids quickly spread north through South America and Central America. They reached Texas in 1990. Today they have spread to the Southwest, the lower Midwest regions of the United States, and Florida.

Unlike their gentle European relatives, the Africanized honeybees are easily startled. They protect their nests fiercely. They can sense vibrations from people or animals more than 50 feet (15 m) from their nests. Once disturbed, swarms of bees may pursue their victims for more than 0.25 mile (0.4 km). Like ordinary honeybees, the Africanized honeybees sting only once. Their **venom** is no more harmful than the venom of ordinary honeybees. But the sheer number of stings from a swarm of angry Africanized honeybees—as many as 1,000—can be deadly. This behavior has earned the Africanized honeybee the nickname "killer bee."

The Africanized bees compete with European honeybees. They mate with European queens and take over their hives. The problems in handling the hives of these aggressive bees has led some people to give up beekeeping.

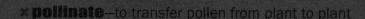

× **pollinate**—to transfer pollen from plant to plant

× **venom**—a poisonous liquid produced by some animals

ASIAN TIGER MOSQUITO

In 1985 a pesky insect arrived in Houston, Texas. The Asian tiger mosquito was found in shipments of used tires from its home in Asia. Others came to California in 2001 in a shipment of bamboo plants.

The Asian tiger mosquito lives only four to six weeks. It rarely flies more than the distance of a few football fields. Even so, it has managed to spread to 26 U.S. states. It makes its home in just about anything that holds standing water, from flower pots to tin cans. When these items get moved around, the mosquitoes move with them.

Asian tiger mosquitoes are especially pesky because they tend to live around humans. Like other mosquitoes, they can spread deadly diseases, such as West Nile virus, to animals and people.

SPREADING DISEASE

Diseases can spread quickly through mosquito bites. For example, if a mosquito carrying the West Nile virus bites a robin, it can pass the virus to the robin. Once infected with the virus, the robin can pass it to other mosquitoes that bite it. Those infected pests can bite other animals and people, infecting them as well.

• The Asian tiger mosquito gets its name from its stripes.

25

CHAPTER FIVE
SOLUTIONS

The best way to deal with the problem of invasive species is to stop them from invading in the first place. U.S. government officials are improving inspections of airplanes, ships, cargo, and baggage that cross the country's borders. Specially trained sniffer dogs can detect all sorts of invaders. They can find brown tree snakes in cargo holds. They can also sniff out plant material that may carry disease.

There are strict laws about what people can bring into the United States or carry across state lines. For example, people can no longer bring Burmese pythons into the United States. It is against the law to carry live Asian carp from one state to another.

Some dogs are specially trained to detect invasive species.

Scientists are looking for new ways to get rid of—or at least control—invasive species. One approach has been to bring in the invader's natural predator. That's what was done to control the red imported fire ant. But scientists have to be very careful. They have to control the species brought in to wipe out the invasive species. Otherwise, the new species could become an invasive species.

ALERT

HELP STOP THE SPREAD OF
NEW ZEALAND MUDSNAILS AND OTHER
AQUATIC NUISANCE SPECIES.

● DISINFECT YOUR FISHING WADERS
AND EQUIPMENT IN THIS TUB. ●

A SOLUTION OF 50/50 FORMULA 409
AND WATER WILL KILL THESE ORGANISMS,
AS WILL WATER TEMPERATURES GREATER THAN
140 OR FREEZING TEMPERATURES FOR
8 HOURS OR LONGER

● A fisherman scrubs his waders and equipment to prevent the spread of invasive species.

DISINFECT
YOUR EQUIPMENT
BEFORE ENTERING
CLUB WATER

HANDLING INVASIVE SPECIES

Invasive species damage the environment, disrupt ecoystems, and cause serious health problems. They cost people billions of dollars each year. The good news is that people can pitch in to help stop the spread of invasive species.

WHAT YOU CAN DO TO STOP THE SPREAD OF INVASIVE SPECIES

• Educate yourself about invasive species in your area. The United States Department of Agriculture's National Invasive Species Information Center provides information about invasive species across the country.

• Help clear any invasive plants in your backyard.

• Never release a pet or aquarium fish into the wild, even if you can't take care of it anymore. It's not fair to your pet, and it can be a disaster for the environment. Take it to an animal shelter where professionals can find it a new home.

• Help keep invasive species contained to one area. Keep watch while outdoors for any plants or animals that want to hitch a ride. Clean all plants and animals such as barnacles and shellfish from boats and gear after fishing. Clean your shoes after hiking.

• If you and your family travel outside the country, don't bring home plants or animals as souvenirs.

GLOSSARY

ecosystem (EE-koh-sis-tuhm)—a system of living and nonliving things in an environment

extinct (ik-STINGKT)—no longer living; an extinct animal is one that has died out, with no more of its kind

habitat (HAB-uh-tat)—the natural place and conditions in which an animal or plant lives

larva (LAR-vuh)—an insect at the stage of development between an egg and an adult; larvae is plural for larva

microbe (MYE-krobe)—a living thing that is too small to see without a microscope

native (NAY-tuhv)—describes a species that lives and grows naturally in a particular region without the help of humans

pollinate (pol-uh-NAYT)—to transfer pollen from plant to plant; pollen makes new plants grow

predator (PRED-uh-tur)—an animal that hunts other animals for food

species (SPEE-sheez)—a group of living things that share common characteristics

venom (VEN-uhm)—a poisonous liquid produced by some animals

READ MORE

Hartman, Eve, and Wendy Meshbesher. *What Is the Threat of Invasive Species?* Chicago: Raintree, 2012.

Jackson, Cari. *Alien Invasion: Invasive Species Become Major Menaces.* Pleasantville, N.Y.: Gareth Stevens Pub., 2010.

Metz, Lorijo. *What Can We Do about Invasive Species?* New York: PowerKids Press, 2010.

INTERNET SITES

FactHound offers a safe, fun way to find Internet sites related to this book. All of the sites on FactHound have been researched by our staff.

Here's all you do:

Visit *www.facthound.com*

Type in this code: 9781476501406

Check out projects, games and lots more at
www.capstonekids.com

INDEX